GW01336146

Original title:
Whispers of Winter

Copyright © 2024 Swan Charm
All rights reserved.

Author: Aron Pilviste
ISBN HARDBACK: 978-9916-79-732-7
ISBN PAPERBACK: 978-9916-79-733-4
ISBN EBOOK: 978-9916-79-734-1

Echoes in the Flurry

Snowflakes fall in whispered grace,
Dancing through the quiet space.
Softly landing, white as night,
Chilling winds in gentle flight.

Branches sway, a silent tune,
Beneath the watchful winter moon.
Footsteps crunch in crisp delight,
Echoes form within the night.

Haunting Melodies of a Numbed Earth

Barren fields, a ghostly scene,
Cold and stark, where life once green.
Whispers linger, tales untold,
Memories in the air unfold.

Frosted winds that carry love,
Murmurs from the stars above.
Nature's breath now still and low,
Haunting melodies of woe.

Prism of the Winter Light

Sunrise spills a liquid hue,
Painting skies in shades anew.
Icicles like crystals shine,
Reflecting warmth in bitter pine.

Colors dance on frosted ground,
Whispers of the light abound.
In this prism, beauty glows,
Winter's art in quiet shows.

Chilled Whispers Underneath

Beneath the snow, a pulse resides,
Life beneath in silence hides.
Chilled whispers, secrets deep,
Dreams that wait and gently sleep.

Nature's heart, though frozen tight,
Wears a cloak of purest white.
In the dark, still lives the spark,
Waiting for the thaw to mark.

Radiance in the Frost

Crystalline whispers dance on land,
Effervescent sparkles, nature's hand.
Each flake a story, delicate and bright,
Turning the world into a canvas of light.

The breath of winter, soft and clear,
Brewing a magic filled with cheer.
Branches adorned with a silvery sheen,
A glimpse of wonder, serene and pristine.

The horizon glows with a gentle blush,
Where time stands still in a sparkling hush.
Crisp air carries dreams of warmth ahead,
In the frosty embrace where shadows tread.

The Unseen Art of the Blizzard

Canvas of white, wild and untamed,
Snowflakes swirl, each uniquely named.
The wind's soft melody, whispers unseen,
Crafting a world where nature's supreme.

Vigorous gusts draw an icy line,
Transforming the mundane to a realm divine.
While silence reigns, the heart beats strong,
In the tempest's dance, the pulse of song.

Picturesque chaos, beauty unchained,
In the blizzard's grip, dreams are refrained.
Each flurry a brushstroke, vivid and bold,
Painting a story in hues of cold.

Secrets of the Shivering Pines

In the still of night, where shadows creep,
Pines wear their cloaks of frost and sleep.
A whisper of secrets, old as time,
Rooted in tales, in breeze and rhyme.

Beneath their boughs, stories unfold,
Of winters past and winters told.
Cacophony of silence, a gentle reprieve,
In the shivering pines, we dare to believe.

Each needle a witness to tales of yore,
Echoes of laughter, wind, and more.
Guardians of wonder, strong and free,
Their whispers invite us to simply be.

Candlelight in the Chill

Flickering wicks in the gathering night,
Casting warm beams in the cold's tight bite.
A glow of hope in winter's embrace,
Candlelight dances with gentle grace.

The world outside, a tapestry grey,
While within these walls, shadows play.
Stories are shared by the flickering flame,
In the calm of the quiet, we're never the same.

Soft whispers linger as embers dim,
Illuminating paths where dreams begin.
With each soft flicker, a memory spun,
Binding our hearts 'til the night is done.

Secrets in the Snow

Whispers in the winter air,
Softly dance like dreams laid bare.
Footprints hidden, trails erased,
In the silence, secrets chased.

Gentle flakes like feathers fall,
Covering the earth, a shroud so tall.
Each crystal holds a story tight,
Invisible truths in the moonlight.

Branches bow with heavy grace,
Nature wears a frozen face.
Crisp and quiet, the world sleeps,
In the snow, a secret keeps.

Echoes linger, soft and low,
In the heart of falling snow.
Listen close, the night will share,
Whispers of a world laid bare.

Hushed Beneath the Snowflakes

In the still of wintry night,
Snowflakes fall, a silver light.
Nature wrapped in purest white,
Hushed and calm, a magical sight.

Beneath this quilt, the earth does dream,
Gentle as a softest gleam.
Silent wishes drift and twirl,
In the peace, new hopes unfurl.

Frosted branches kiss the sky,
As the moon begins to sigh.
Memories dance in the cold air,
Hushed beneath the snowflakes' care.

Every flake a tale to tell,
In the night, all is well.
Close your eyes, let worries fade,
In this hush, a promise made.

Glistening Shadows

Night descends with velvet grace,
Glistening shadows start to trace.
Moonlight spills on winter's face,
In this scene, we find our place.

Frosty whispers through the trees,
Caught in time, like gentle breeze.
Silence hums a tranquil tune,
As stars twinkle, bright as noon.

Every shimmer, every gleam,
Paints the world in silver dream.
Shadows play, they twist and twine,
In the night, all hearts align.

With each breath, the night grows deep,
In these glistening dreams, we leap.
Through the dark, we find our way,
In glistening shadows, we will stay.

Lullabies of the Frost

Softly falls the winter chill,
Lullabies the night does spill.
Frosty fingers, sweet embrace,
Nature sings in quiet grace.

In the quiet, hearts will sigh,
Underneath the starry sky.
Snowflakes whisper, dreams take flight,
Holding warmth within the night.

Each breath of cold, a fleeting note,
Melodies the frost will quote.
Dancing dreams upon the air,
In this lullaby, we share.

So let the winter's song be heard,
In the silence, feel each word.
Wrapped in peace, let worries fade,
In lullabies, our fears allayed.

A Canvas of White

Blanket of snow spread wide,
Soft whispers in the light,
Fields dressed in frosty pride,
Nature's canvas, pure and bright.

Footprints etched in silence,
A child's laughter fills the air,
Joy dances in the stillness,
Winter's magic everywhere.

Birch trees stand like sentries,
Guarding secrets of the night,
Branches draped like memories,
In the glow of pale moonlight.

The world wraps in slumber,
Beneath the shimmering sky,
Time moves in gentle numbers,
As dreams begin to fly.

In this serene, quiet scene,
Hope's reflection can be found,
A canvas of soft, white sheen,
Peace in every flake that's crowned.

The Veil of the December Night

Stars like diamonds twinkle high,
In the vault of frosty air,
Whispers of the night softly sigh,
Under the sky's calm glare.

Trees wear coats of silver sheen,
Moonlight bathes the world below,
A tranquil beauty, rare and clean,
Wrapped in winter's gentle glow.

Footsteps echo in the dark,
With every crunch, a tale unfolds,
In this quiet, sacred park,
Dreams and visions, brave and bold.

The chill wraps close, yet feels so right,
As moments dance in tranquil bliss,
Embracing the magic of the night,
In every shadow, a tender kiss.

Beneath the veil of frosted dreams,
Hope and wonder intertwine,
In stillness deep, life softly gleams,
A canvas where hearts align.

The Cloak of Frost

Morning dew like diamonds gleam,
A cloak of frost on every leaf,
Nature whispers, day's new theme,
In quiet moments, find belief.

The world awakens slow and sweet,
Breath of winter fills the air,
Each step, where frost and grass meet,
Silent footprints everywhere.

Sunrise paints the sky in gold,
Chasing away the night's embrace,
Stories of warmth, silently told,
As joy brings life to this cold space.

With every heartbeat, nature sighs,
The cloak of frost begins to thaw,
Underneath, a world that cries,
For warmth to break the winter's law.

In this dance of cold and light,
Hope's whisper stirs within the dark,
The cloak of frost, a fleeting sight,
Where dreams ignite their tiny spark.

Echoes Under the Snow

Whispers trace the frozen ground,
Silent echoes fill the air,
Underneath, the secrets found,
Winter's story hidden there.

Branches creak with ancient tales,
Of seasons past, love, and strife,
A world where every heartbeat pales,
Yet beats anew with vibrant life.

In the stillness, time stands still,
Memories drift like snowflakes' flight,
Each breath a promise, hopes fulfill,
Beneath the endless, starry night.

Snowflakes fall like softest dreams,
Painting thoughts in purest white,
In this world where nothing seems,
But beauty shines in the moonlight.

Echoes linger, gentle sighs,
Underneath the winter's glow,
In a silence, love never dies,
For all is known in the snow.

Chilling Echoes

In the distance, shadows play,
Whispers dance on winds so gray.
Frozen breath of winter's might,
Echoes linger through the night.

Beneath the stars, secrets sigh,
Crisp silence where soft dreams lie.
Moonlight flickers, gleams like glass,
Memories of the moments past.

Frosted branches, lightly bowed,
Nature's cloak, a tranquil shroud.
Softly, softly, night unfolds,
Tales untold in whispers cold.

Time stands still, a haunting tune,
Chill of twilight, light of moon.
Embers fade in warming light,
Chilling echoes last the night.

Footsteps fade on falling snow,
In the silence, feelings grow.
Hearts entwined, a subtle thread,
In the echoes, hopes are fed.

Murmurs of the North

Winds arise, a constant drift,
Nature whispers, gentle gift.
Mountains stand with ancient grace,
In their shadows, hearts find space.

Rivers flow with stories deep,
Murmurs beckon, dawn asleep.
Pine trees sway, a lullaby,
In their arms, the spirits fly.

Northern lights paint skies aglow,
Mystic colors swirl and flow.
Across the tundra, soft and wide,
Dreams awaken, spirits glide.

Cold embraces, warm hearts thrive,
In this magic, we arrive.
Through the storms, we find our way,
Murmurs guide, come what may.

Stars above in watchful gaze,
Facing through the moonlit haze.
With each dawn, new tales are spun,
In the North, our hearts are one.

Veils of Ice

Frosted panes like whispered dreams,
Silent shadows softly gleam.
Veils of ice, a world so bright,
Hiding secrets from the light.

Crystals form on every branch,
Nature's art in every chance.
Frozen lakes, reflections freeze,
Captured moments in the breeze.

Winter's breath, a ghostly touch,
Chill of night, it says so much.
Underneath the silver glow,
Veils of ice conceal the flow.

Hidden realms where spirits dwell,
In the silence, stories swell.
Moonlight casts its gentle gaze,
Through the veils, in quiet haze.

Beneath the frost, the earth will sleep,
In its heart, the dreams we keep.
Nature's breath, a quiet fight,
Through the veils, we find the light.

Shimmering Silence

In the dawn, a silver glow,
Shimmering silence starts to flow.
Fields of gold where shadows play,
In the stillness, dreams array.

Softly now, the world awakes,
Gentle breeze through grasses shakes.
Morning light upon the stream,
Whispers flow like fleeting dream.

Through the woods, a calm embrace,
Nature's cradle, sacred space.
Hushed reflections, pearls of dew,
Sparkling silence, waking new.

Every leaf a gentle sigh,
Together, earth and sky comply.
In this moment, pure and bright,
Shimmering silence feels just right.

Time pauses, heartbeats blend,
In this realm, we transcend.
With each breath, we find our place,
In shimmering silence, human grace.

Shadows in the Chill

In the night, the shadows creep,
Silent whispers, secrets deep.
Frosty breath upon the air,
A shiver trails, a chill laid bare.

Moonlight dances on the ground,
Hushed, the world is wrapped around.
Crystals glisten, stars align,
In the stillness, hearts entwine.

Branches bare, like bated breath,
Nature waits, a watch for death.
Yet in darkness, hope shall twine,
As shadows weave, a thread divine.

Footfalls echo on the snow,
Memories buried, long ago.
Each step holds a fleeting spark,
Guided softly through the dark.

When dawn breaks, the chill will fade,
Yet in silence, dreams are made.
For every shadow speaks the truth,
In winter's heart, we find our youth.

Unseen Songs of December

Beneath the weight of winter's cloak,
Quiet notes and memories spoke.
Branches sway in icy breeze,
Nature hums her hidden pleas.

Scattered wishes, drifting far,
Hopes and dreams like falling stars.
While frost bites, the hearth glows bright,
Warmth encircles the quiet night.

Crisp and clear, the world awakes,
In the hush, a stillness breaks.
Songs of laughter, slightly blurred,
In the cold, not one word heard.

Chill of twilight, shadows cast,
Whispers carried through the past.
Unseen worlds in silver light,
December sings, a soft delight.

As time passes, moments blend,
Every heartbeat knows no end.
In the silence, life renews,
Unseen songs are ours to choose.

Twilight of the Frost

When twilight drapes the world in gray,
Frost creeps in to softly sway.
Colors fade to cold embrace,
In the stillness, we find space.

Glistening crystals fall like tears,
Each one holds our hopes and fears.
Nature whispers secrets low,
In the twilight, all things grow.

Stars emerge from icy shroud,
Proud and fierce, they pierce the cloud.
Quiet magic in the night,
Guides the wanderers into light.

Every shadow, every sigh,
Echoes tales of days gone by.
In this moment, time stands still,
As frost's touch bends to our will.

In the chill, our spirits soar,
Through the twilight, we explore.
For in the frost, we find our way,
To brighter dawns of every day.

Echoes of a Frozen Heart

In the silence, echoes play,
Frozen beats, a heart's ballet.
Whispers linger, soft and low,
In the frost, true feelings grow.

Longing stirs with every breath,
In the stillness, glimmers of depth.
Shadows dance, a quiet game,
Each heartbeat calls an ancient name.

The cold wraps tight, a velvet shroud,
Isolation in the crowd.
Yet within that biting chill,
Warmth awakens, an upward thrill.

Frozen dreams begin to thaw,
Tender moments, hearts in awe.
In the echoes of the night,
Hope emerges into light.

With every pulse, with every sigh,
Through the darkness, we can fly.
For in our hearts, a fire burns,
From frozen dreams, our world returns.

Beneath the Blanket of Snow

Silent whispers in the night,
Covering earth in purest white.
Softly falling, dreams take flight,
Beneath the stars, a tranquil sight.

Gentle flakes, they swirl and weave,
Nature's quilt, a gift we cleave.
In this hush, we dare to believe,
Winter's charm, we gladly receive.

Footprints marked on frosty ground,
Echoing sounds, a peace profound.
Within the stillness, joy is found,
Nature's heart, in silence bound.

Branches draped in crystal lace,
A fleeting glimpse of magic's grace.
Every flake, a secret place,
In snowy realms, time slows its pace.

As dawn breaks, the world aglow,
Colors blend with the melting snow.
Beneath the blanket, life will grow,
In winter's hold, our spirits flow.

Hidden Voices in the Cold

In twilight's grip, the shadows creep,
Voices linger, secrets keep.
Frozen air, the stillness deep,
Whispers wake while others sleep.

Beneath the ice, the stories lie,
Frozen dreams that drift and sigh.
In the silence, hear the cry,
Life beneath the coldest sky.

Echoes trace the paths we tread,
Silent murmurs of the dead.
Every flake, a tale unspreads,
In the cold, their voices spread.

Frosted winds, they weave a song,
Tales of right, the tales of wrong.
In the night, where hearts belong,
Hidden voices call us strong.

With each gust, a memory stirs,
Through the freeze, the past occurs.
In the chill, the heart endures,
Hidden voices, winter purrs.

Breezes of Stillness

Whispers float on winter's air,
Gently kissed, the world laid bare.
In the calm, a tender care,
Breezes dance with soft despair.

Echoes trail the falling snow,
Murmurs caught in twilight's glow.
Nature's breath, a tranquil flow,
In the stillness, time moves slow.

Branches sway, the silence hums,
Breezes carry soft low drums.
In this hush, a feeling comes,
The heart in quiet rhythm strums.

Frosted pathways lie ahead,
In the chill, where dreams are fed.
Breezes whisper what's unsaid,
In stillness, love and hope are bred.

As dusk descends, the stars will chime,
Nature holds its sacred rhyme.
In every breeze, a sense of time,
In stillness, all is truly prime.

Echoes of a Snowbound Tale

A tale unfolds in winter's grasp,
Each flake a story, soft to clasp.
Echoing dreams in every rasp,
In the quiet, memories clasp.

Snowflakes dance on silent ground,
Whirling whispers all around.
In the frost, truths can be found,
Echoes linger, profound sound.

With each sigh of frosty air,
The heart remembers, thick with care.
Voices lost, but always there,
In the hush, we pause and share.

Hidden trails through shades of white,
Lost in dreams, we seek the light.
Snowbound echoes, our delight,
A wondrous tale in purest sight.

As the night envelops all,
Softest blankets hear the call.
In the echo, we stand tall,
United in this snowbound thrall.

Hushed Nights Beneath the Stars

In the silence of the night, bright stars gleam,
Whispers of the cosmos weave through every dream.
Moonlight dances softly on the twilight's face,
In this tranquil moment, we find our place.

Cool breezes sweep across the open land,
Nature's beauty speaks, a language so grand.
Every heartbeat echoes in the stillness deep,
Hushed secrets among us, a promise we keep.

Beneath the vast canvas, our souls intertwine,
Painting dreams with glimmers, like a gentle sign.
Time suspends its march in this sacred space,
Hushed nights beneath stars, a warm embrace.

As constellations shimmer, stories unfold,
Carried by the night, their beauty untold.
The universe listens to our whispered delight,
In the hush of the night, love takes flight.

Let's savor the magic of moments so rare,
Binding our hearts in the cool night air.
Forever we'll cherish this time 'neath the sky,
In hushed nights together, we silently fly.

Secrets of the Sleet

Falling gently, the sleet knows well,
Each crystal carries a story to tell.
Whispers of winter in chilly embrace,
Secrets of the sleet, a hidden place.

Softly it blankets the world all around,
Covering echoes, muffling the sound.
In this shivering silence, mysteries grow,
Sleet keeps its secrets, only it will know.

Beneath the frozen veil, dreams might still gleam,
Hope twinkles quietly, like a fleeting dream.
Glistening whispers caress the cold air,
Seeking solace in the secrets we share.

The pathways of ice lead where few have tread,
In a world hushed by winter, our hearts are fed.
In the dance of the sleet, we find our own way,
Carving memories softly as night turns to day.

With each flake that falls, a new tale is born,
In the heart of the cold, there's warmth to adorn.
As we walk through the sleet, hand in hand so tight,
Secrets of the season shine brilliantly bright.

Tranquil Happenings in the Cold

Snowflakes drift gently, a soft lullaby,
Covering the earth with a delicate sigh.
In the heart of the cold, peace finds its way,
Tranquil happenings warm the winter's gray.

Children laugh joyously, crafting their dreams,
Building tiny castles where hope softly gleams.
Every moment echoes in the frosty air,
In the hush of the cold, magic is rare.

Footprints in snow tell stories of play,
Guiding us forward as the light fades away.
Underneath the stillness, life's rhythm remains,
In tranquil happenings, love's whisper sustains.

The world is a canvas, serene and bright,
Colored by laughter that dances with light.
In chilly adventures, connections unfold,
Tranquil happenings worth more than gold.

As twilight embraces the day's gentle close,
Winter's soft breath lingers, a delicate prose.
Wrapped in the stillness, we cherish the old,
In the beauty of winter, our hearts are consoled.

The Language of Ice and Snow

Listen closely, the world begins to speak,
In whispers of ice, its message unique.
Each snowflake a note in winter's cruel song,
The language of snow where we all belong.

Nature's chorus carries through cold, crisp air,
Melodies of silence, a soothing affair.
In every crackle, the ice tells the past,
Tales of soft moments, memories amassed.

Frosted branches twinkle under moonlight's grace,
Painting dreams in white in this sacred space.
The language of frost, both gentle and bold,
A tapestry woven, stories retold.

In the heart of winter, beneath the night's glow,
A symphony rises in the hush of the snow.
With every step taken, nature unfolds,
The language of ice in mysteries holds.

So let us embrace the chill in the air,
Communicating softly, a bond we will share.
In the beauty of winter, hear the call flow,
The language of ice and snow, pure as snow.

Frostbitten Fables

In whispered tales the cold winds sigh,
Stories of dreams where winter birds fly.
Branches wear cloaks of shimmering white,
Fables spun softly in the silent night.

Frozen streams murmur secrets to the land,
Each snowflake a letter in time's gentle hand.
Footprints lead where the wild things dwell,
In frostbitten fables, enchantments compel.

A solitary fox trails through the trees,
Braving the chill with agile ease.
Stars twinkle bright in the victory fight,
Against the moon's reign, a glorious night.

Firewood crackles, a warm glowing light,
Casting shadows that dance in delight.
With every ember, stories ignite,
Frostbitten fables take flight in the night.

Echoing Lullabies of the Season

Softly the snowflakes begin to descend,
Whispers of comfort, a lullaby's blend.
Nature unfolds in a blanket of peace,
As time slows down, and the worries cease.

Night sings of silence, a soothing refrain,
Stars join the melody, bright in the rain.
Each breath is a hush, a soft winter kiss,
Years dance along to this magical bliss.

Trees sway gently to the tunes of the night,
Crickets are quiet, their songs take flight.
Under the moon's gentle glow, we dream,
Of echoing lullabies wrapped in moonbeam.

Drift on the currents of soft snowy flakes,
While shadows embrace in the stillness that breaks.
Lost in the warmth of this beautiful scene,
Echoing lullabies, peaceful and serene.

The Calm Before the Blizzard

A hush so profound, a pause in the air,
Winter prepares with delicate care.
Last light of twilight fades out of sight,
While whispering winds weave the fabric of night.

Frost on the windows, a shimmering veil,
Nature awaits the great, swirling gale.
Animals nestle, embracing the gloom,
Inside the warm heart that ready to bloom.

Clouds gather slowly, a blanket of gray,
The world holds its breath for the cold's grand display.
Icicles form with a glinting allure,
The calm before chaos, a moment so pure.

Beneath the still sky, there's magic in wait,
Anticipation builds, a delicate fate.
An orchestra playing, each note rich and grand,
The calm before the storm, a whispering hand.

Fragments of a Frosty Morn

Dewdrops glisten on blades of grass,
As morning's light bids the night to pass.
A canvas of silver greets the new day,
In fragments of frost, all they convey.

Each breath is a cloud, catching the chill,
Nature awakens with magical thrill.
Trees stand adorned in a crystal embrace,
Framing the dawn with a wintry grace.

Footsteps crunch softly on pathways unknown,
Guided by whispers, all softly intone.
Moments unfold like petals in bloom,
Fragments of life in the frosty morn's loom.

The sun stretches slowly, dispelling the fears,
Melting the ice that clings through the years.
A day filled with promise, as colors take form,
In fragments of beauty, where hearts keep warm.

The Gentle Touch of Frosted Air

A whisper soft, the night descends,
Its breath a chill, the world it mends.
Each blade of grass, a crystal lance,
In silver light, the shadows dance.

The stars above, they twinkle bright,
In the embrace of frosted night.
A tranquil hush upon the ground,
In this stillness, peace is found.

The air bites gently, crisp and clear,
It carries secrets, whispers near.
With every breath, it sparkles light,
A fleeting kiss, in cold's delight.

Trees wear coats of frosty white,
Their limbs adorned, a pure delight.
Nature sleeps, yet breathes in grace,
In winter's arms, a warm embrace.

So let the world in silence bloom,
As frosted air dispels the gloom.
In gentle touch, the cold inspires,
A heart ignited, warmed by fires.

A Reverie of Ice-Covered Fields

Fields stretch wide, a gleaming sheet,
Crisp reflections beneath our feet.
A tapestry of white and blue,
Nature's canvas, fresh and new.

Each frozen step, a crunch, a cheer,
Echoes of dreams that linger near.
In this expanse, the spirit flies,
As every breath sparks winter's sighs.

The sun peeks forth, a timid glow,
Kissing the frost that glimmers slow.
A fleeting warmth that knows no bounds,
In crystal charm, serenity sounds.

The silence wraps the world in peace,
While frozen moments seem to cease.
A realm untouched, where time stands still,
In ice-bound dreams, we find our will.

So wander forth, let visions bloom,
In reveries that chase the gloom.
For in these fields, life's magic glows,
As winter's heart within us grows.

Dreaming Beneath a Frozen Canopy

Underneath the branches bare,
Dreams unfold in frosted air.
A canopy of ice and light,
Cradles visions through the night.

Snowflakes drift like whispered lies,
In slumber deep, the world complies.
Each flake a wish, a silent prayer,
In this stillness, hearts lay bare.

Stars peek through the frozen boughs,
In nature's grip, we find our vows.
A promise wrapped in sparkling frost,
In dreams beneath, no hope is lost.

The moonlight weaves a silver thread,
Guiding souls where angels tread.
A gentle hush, a lullaby,
As time stands still, beneath the sky.

So dream with me, the night unfurls,
In frozen realms, our hearts twirl.
Beneath the canopy, we belong,
In winter's arms, we sing our song.

Light in the Depths of the Cold

Amidst the chill, a glow appears,
A beacon bright, it calms our fears.
In darkest nights, a spark ignites,
With warmth that dances, soft delights.

The snow may fall, the world turns white,
Yet deep within, we find the light.
Each flicker glows against the dark,
A flame of hope, a tender spark.

The frost may bite, the winds may howl,
Yet in our hearts, we wear a vow.
To seek the light, to cherish warmth,
As life's great waves, we brave the storm.

With hands held tight, we face the cold,
Our bonds, a warmth that won't grow old.
In unity, our spirits soar,
For in the depths, we find much more.

So let the winter winds arise,
We'll find the light beneath the skies.
In every breath, in every heart,
We're never lost, we play our part.

Secrets of the Icy Woods

Whispers linger in the air,
Beneath branches cold and bare.
Shadows dance with silent grace,
Nature's secrets find their place.

Glimmers shine on frozen leaves,
As frosty winds weave through the eaves.
Hidden paths where no one goes,
The heart of winter gently glows.

Footsteps echo, soft and light,
In a world draped in silver-white.
Mysteries wrapped in a soft quilt,
Of icy wonder, dreams are built.

Animals seek their hidden den,
Traces lost, but found again.
All around, a magical sight,
In the depths of the longest night.

Frosty Footprints

Footprints etched in glistening snow,
Guiding paths where cold winds blow.
Each step whispers tales untold,
Secrets of the brave and bold.

With each crunch beneath my feet,
Echoes of the wild retreat.
Frozen air, a chill that bites,
Keeps the secrets of the nights.

Animals roam, silent and shy,
Watching as the shadows fly.
Hidden worlds beneath the frost,
In winter's grasp, we seek the lost.

Light fades soft, the moon ascends,
Illuminating where the trail bends.
In the stillness, magic stirs,
Frosty footprints, the world concurs.

The night unveils a crystal view,
Where dreams and reality renew.
In frosty whispers, life begins,
The dance of winter, where time spins.

Tales Carved in Ice

Sculpted stories, nature's grace,
Ice reveals a hidden place.
Each formation tells a tale,
In the stillness, breezes sail.

Crystal rivers, frozen streams,
Reflecting softly winter's dreams.
Shapes emerge from frosty breath,
Echoes of life, and hints of death.

Carved in silence, sharp and clear,
Every block holds what we fear.
Yet beauty glows, a gleaming sight,
Tales entwined in purest light.

A frozen world, serene and bright,
Holds the magic of the night.
In every shard, a fleeting glance,
Of forgotten dreams, a whispered chance.

Together, nature weaves and spins,
Telling tales of losses, wins.
In the winter's breath we find,
The stories carved, forever bind.

Enigmas of the Long Night

Stars twinkle in the frozen air,
 A blanket of silence everywhere.
  Shadows murmur secrets low,
 Beneath the glimmering, icy glow.

 Time stands still in endless dark,
   Each flicker ignites a spark.
 Whispers flow through trees so tall,
   Enigmas linger, quietly call.

The moon's pale light, a guiding hand,
  Leading dreams to distant land.
 In ghostly forms, the night expands,
Touching hearts with gentle strands.

 Memories rise like vapor trails,
   Stories woven into the gales.
  Silence deepens, worlds collide,
In the shadows where thoughts reside.

 From the depths, a wisdom speaks,
  As the night reveals what seeks.
   In the dark, we find our way,
   Enigmas of night lead to day.

The Secrets Between the Snow and Sky

Whispers of the winter breeze,
Dance softly through the pines.
Crisp flakes scatter in the air,
Each one a tale that twines.

Veils of white cloak the still ground,
Silent steps on a frozen path.
Footprints fade without a sound,
A fleeting moment's aftermath.

Clouds above wear a gown of grey,
The sun peeks, shy and bright.
In the hush of the falling day,
Secrets hide in the fading light.

The world wrapped in a quiet shroud,
Hushed echoes of a deep breath.
Each flake adorned with a dream allowed,
Winter's beauty, a dance with death.

Beneath the snow, life waits tight,
Holding on through the chill.
In the heart of the winter night,
New wonders are born, still.

Twilight's Embrace in the Still Cold

Twilight cloaks the world in blue,
As shadows stretch and sigh.
The cold breathes gentle and true,
Kissing the earth and sky.

Stars flicker in their lonesome places,
Frosty whispers roam.
Embracing all the hidden spaces,
In winter's tranquil home.

The moon hangs low, a silver thread,
Weaving dreams in the dark.
Silent stories long since said,
Kindling a timid spark.

Each breath a cloud that floats away,
Dancing in the night.
Where the heart finds pause to stay,
Wrapped in the soft twilight.

Echoes linger on the chill,
Adrift on winds of time.
In the night, the world is still,
Held in winter's rhyme.

Whispers Beneath the Ice

Underneath the frozen sheet,
Life stirs in a muffled way.
Voices muffled, soft and sweet,
Beneath the icy sway.

Roots weave gently, seeking light,
Through the chilling, blue haze.
Dreams wrapped tight in the silent night,
Hope held in quiet ways.

Crystals form with a tender touch,
An art where time stands still.
Each fracture holds a secret, such,
In echoes of winter's thrill.

The world above wears a frosty crown,
But warmth beats hidden and bold.
Beneath the ice, life won't back down,
Resilient, its story told.

In the stillness, whispers thrive,
A symphony of hope.
Beneath the ice, the heart's alive,
In the dance of silent scope.

The Soft Song of Cold Evenings

Cold evenings bring a gentle song,
Of whispers that melt the night.
A symphony where hearts belong,
Wrapped in the perfect light.

Candles flicker with tender grace,
Casting shadows on the wall.
Embracing warmth in our space,
The soft glow holds us all.

Outside the world begins to freeze,
Each breath is a swirling ghost.
Inside we find our hearts at ease,
With joys we cherish most.

Laughter mingles with the chill,
In cozy corners where we meet.
Every moment, time stands still,
Life's tapestry, complete.

A soft song drifts on the breeze,
Notes of love and content.
In these evenings, the heart finds peace,
Rich with a sweet lament.

Ethereal Hues in the Darkness

In twilight's gentle, fading light,
Shadows blend with colors bright.
Whispers dance upon the breeze,
Painting dreams among the trees.

Stars awaken, twinkling shy,
As night unfolds its velvet sky.
Each hue a promise, soft and rare,
A canvas brushed with tender care.

Moonlight mingles with the desire,
Setting hearts and souls afire.
In the depths, where secrets lie,
Ethereal hues of a midnight sigh.

Nature hums a lullaby sweet,
Where darkness and colors meet.
In the stillness, magic found,
With each heartbeat, grace surrounds.

So linger here, in twilight's embrace,
Where dreams and shadows interlace.
Let the night be a soothing balm,
In ethereal hues, we find our calm.

A Gathering of Frosted Memories

In crystal air, the whispers call,
Frosted memories, one and all.
Each breath a cloud, a fleeting trace,
In winter's grip, a perfect space.

Echoes of laughter fill the cold,
Tales of warmth and moments told.
Beneath the frost, a story flows,
Of cherished times when love still glows.

Icicles hang like dreams on string,
Awaiting tales that winter brings.
In every flake, a past entwined,
A gathering of hearts, aligned.

The world transformed, a silver lace,
Time stands still in this embrace.
Memories breathe, alive and bright,
In the frost's gentle, secret light.

So gather close, let spirits soar,
In frosted moments, evermore.
In every sigh, a chance to mend,
A gathering of memories, no end.

Frosted Breath

A chill escapes with every breath,
In frozen hush, a dance with death.
The world adorned, a crystal sheen,
In winter's grasp, our secrets glean.

Frosted whispers cut the air,
Fragile echoes, everywhere.
Each tiny shard, a frozen tear,
Bestowed with dreams, both near and dear.

The morning sun begins its rise,
Casting light on winter skies.
In every frost, a story spun,
A fleeting moment, just begun.

Breathe in deep, the icy glow,
Feel the magic in the snow.
Frosted breaths, alive and clear,
Remind us all that love is near.

So take a moment, pause and sigh,
Appreciate the beauty nigh.
In every breath, the world will dance,
Frosted dreams, a gentle trance.

Silent Snowfall

In silence falls the gentle snow,
A whispered grace, a soft hello.
Each flake unique, a work of art,
Cascades of white, they touch the heart.

With each descent, the world anew,
Blanketed in thoughts so true.
A hush that quiets all the strife,
In silent snowfall, whispers life.

Trees wear crowns of purest lace,
Nature's touch, a warm embrace.
Steps are muffled, soft and light,
In this moment, all feels right.

Every flake, a wish it brings,
Floating down on feathered wings.
As night descends, the stars align,
In silent snowfall, everything's divine.

So linger here, in winter's glow,
Feel the peace, let worries go.
In the stillness, spirits rise,
In silent snowfall, love complies.

The Frosty Veil

A blanket white spreads far and wide,
Each flake a whisper, nature's pride.
Trees like ghosts in silver shrouds,
Silent beauty beneath the clouds.

The world holds its breath, wrapped in dreams,
Everything glimmers, or so it seems.
Footprints trace stories on crisp, clean ground,
In this hushed realm, peace can be found.

Icicles hang like chandeliers bright,
Catching the sun with a sparkling light.
The air bites sharp, yet feels sublime,
Time slows down in this frosted clime.

Beneath the Winter Sky

Stars glisten under a canvas of blue,
The moon whispers secrets, known by few.
Snowflakes drift softly, a delicate dance,
In shadows of night, the world finds romance.

Fires crackle warmly, stories unfold,
While outside, the world is silent and cold.
Each breath appears as a misty sigh,
Life pauses gently beneath the winter sky.

The chill wraps around like a lover's embrace,
Nature's own stillness, a tranquil space.
Every moment holds magic, peace in the air,
In this quiet realm, there's beauty to share.

A Dance of Ice Crystals

On windowpanes, frost carves its art,
Intricate patterns that capture the heart.
Each crystal unique in its delicate grace,
A fleeting moment in time's warm embrace.

Sunrise paints gold on a silver sheet,
Transforming the land where chill and warmth meet.
Nature sighs softly, a mystical trance,
As the world comes alive with a delicate dance.

Whispers of winter in every light breeze,
Leaves the soul lifted, as if to tease.
A tapestry woven from ice and from fire,
Creating a melody that all hearts inspire.

Hibernal Tranquility

The world lays still in a blanket of snow,
Fields of white where gentle winds blow.
Under soft layers, life quietly sleeps,
Awaiting the spring, as the promise it keeps.

Branches are bare, yet beauty remains,
In the calm of the season, peace gently reigns.
Footprints of silence echo through the day,
As time stretches slowly, in a serene ballet.

The chill of the air wraps around like a shawl,
Snowflakes descend, a soft, soothing call.
In this hibernal nook, the heart learns to rest,
Finding solace in stillness, in nature's own nest.

A Heartbeat Beneath the Frost

In winter's chill, the silence grows,
A heartbeat soft where stillness flows.
Beneath the frost, life holds its breath,
Whispers of warmth amidst the death.

Frozen branches hold the light,
Stars above in silent flight.
A world asleep, yet dreams do swell,
In every flake, a tale to tell.

The moonlight dances on the ground,
In frozen hues, life's pulse is found.
Soft sighs echo in the night,
As shadows weave with gentle light.

Each heartbeat brings a promise near,
Of spring's embrace, of life sincere.
Within the frost, a spark will glow,
A vision bright of what we sow.

So let the cold descend with grace,
For in the dark, we find our place.
Each moment lingers, sweet and true,
A heartbeat waits, to break anew.

Nightfall in the White Realm

As twilight falls, the shadows crawl,
The silent snow begins to call.
A white realm stretches far and wide,
Where dreams and whispers gently hide.

The stars ignite in velvet skies,
A silver moon with watchful eyes.
Each flake a story, drifting slow,
In this enchanted world of snow.

The trees stand tall, silhouettes bare,
Cradling secrets, fragile and rare.
In every rustle, the night unfolds,
A tapestry of tales retold.

Footsteps echo on the frozen ground,
In this stillness, a peace profound.
The world transformed, serene and bright,
Bathed in the glow of the soft moonlight.

So embrace the magic that night bestows,
In the white realm where the stillness flows.
Let your heart wander, let your spirit roam,
For in this night, you find your home.

Echoes Beneath the Snowfall

Beneath the veil of winter's hand,
The world holds secrets, soft and grand.
Echoes whisper in the trees,
Carried gently on the breeze.

Each flake that falls, a memory spun,
Of laughter shared, of races run.
In every drift, a story lies,
Beneath the vast and open skies.

The hush of night, the glow of white,
A tranquil peace, a pure delight.
Footsteps lead to unknown fates,
In the silence that winter creates.

With every breath, the cold bites deep,
Yet in this chill, our hearts will leap.
Embracing echoes, strong and free,
A symphony of harmony.

So heed the snow that wraps us tight,
In its embrace, we find our light.
For in these echoes, pure and bright,
We gather warmth through winter's night.

The Call of Icebound Woods

In the depth of winter, the woods stand tall,
With trunks like giants, they guard us all.
A call of silence, crisp and clear,
Inviting souls to linger near.

The branches glisten, a jeweled crown,
In the icy breath, the world slows down.
Footfalls crunch on the frozen earth,
Where whispers echo of life's rebirth.

The moonlight spills through a veil of frost,
In these woods, no moment is lost.
Each shadow dances, a fleeting wisp,
In the chill of night, we breathe and lisp.

A tale unfolds in the pale moon's glow,
Of hidden paths that only few know.
The call of woods, both wild and free,
Awakens our hearts, sets our spirits free.

So heed the call when the night is deep,
In icebound woods where secrets sleep.
For in this stillness, life starts to weave,
A tapestry of dreams that we believe.

The Unseen Symphony of Cold

Whispers of winter in the air,
Silent notes that melt with care.
A tapestry of frost unfolds,
In hues of silver, dreams retold.

The breath of morning, crystal clear,
A symphony that draws us near.
Each flake a dancer, light and free,
Composing magic, mysteriously.

Nature's chorus, soft and bright,
Plays the solace of the night.
Frosty branches sway and bend,
A melody that will not end.

In every shadow, music flows,
A gentle warmth beneath the snow.
The unseen strings of winter play,
In harmony, they guide the day.

As silence blankets all around,
The heartbeat of the coldest sound.
With every breath, we find the peace,
Of winter's song that never cease.

Treading Lightly on Frost

Footsteps quiet on the ground,
In a world where dreams are found.
Each crunch a soft and fleeting sound,
As nature's hush wraps all around.

A delicate dance begins anew,
Beneath the sky of endless blue.
With every step, a story told,
Of winter's beauty, pure and bold.

Fingers trace the icy hues,
Painting whispers, gentle cues.
With every breath, the frost ignites,
A world transformed by winter's lights.

The sparkle caught in morning's eye,
As sunbeams weave and softly fly.
A moment caught in crisp delight,
Treading lightly, hearts take flight.

Awakening edges, bright and stark,
Where shadows play and whispers hark.
In the stillness, find your way,
Through frosty fields where spirits play.

Silhouettes in Frozen Moments

Beneath the pale, ethereal light,
Shadows dance as day turns night.
Figures merge in stillness found,
Frozen frames where dreams abound.

The world is cast in silver glow,
Hidden stories in the flow.
Every outline tells a tale,
In the quiet, hearts set sail.

Silhouettes in frosted air,
Whispers linger everywhere.
Each breath a painting, crisp and clear,
Ebbing moments, drawing near.

Time stands still as echoes ring,
In the silence, shadows sing.
With every glance, a world is spun,
In frozen moments, we've just begun.

Caught between the dark and light,
Fleeting forms take gentle flight.
In this canvas, life feels whole,
Silhouettes of the heart and soul.

Dreams Inscribed in Snow

Whispers of winter gently fall,
Each flake a story, a silent call.
Footprints dance in soft white hue,
Tracing the paths where dreams come true.

Beneath the blanket, secrets lie,
Echoed hopes beneath the sky.
With each dawn, new tales emerge,
In frosty air, they start to surge.

Winds weave through the barren trees,
Rustling branches, a gentle breeze.
Crystals sparkle in morning light,
A canvas painted pure and bright.

In twilight's glow, shadows blend,
Nature's whispers never end.
The world rests quiet, calm, and slow,
As dreams are inscribed in radiant snow.

Eyes close softly, visions near,
Awakening hopes, both bright and clear.
In every flake, a wish survives,
In winter's embrace, our spirit thrives.

Illuminated by the North Star

Under the vastness of the night,
The North Star glows, a guiding light.
Wandering souls, lost and free,
Find their paths, just wait and see.

Hushed whispers travel on the breeze,
Carried far beyond the trees.
Each glimmer speaks of dreams anew,
In every heart, a spark breaks through.

The moonlight dances on frozen ground,
While silent wonders all around.
Embers of hope in the darkened glade,
In this moment, fears allayed.

Tales of ages long since past,
Under the stars, forever cast.
Stories woven in the night sky,
Where wishes and memories forever lie.

So lift your eyes and heed the call,
The North Star shining over all.
In its glow, our hearts will soar,
Illuminated, forevermore.

Frosty Whimsy

In a world of glimmer and chill,
Frosty whispers, a playful thrill.
Snowflakes twirl in a merry dance,
Inviting all to take a chance.

Glistening branches wear a crown,
Nature's jewels, in white gown.
Children laugh as snowballs fly,
Joyful echoes beneath the sky.

The air is crisp, a fresh delight,
Holding secrets of the night.
Every drift, a chance to play,
In frosty wonders, we lose our way.

Swirls of snow in the twilight glow,
Crafting magic, soft and slow.
Dreams take flight on winter's breath,
In this frosty whimsy, we find depth.

So let us cherish moments shared,
In laughter's echo, we are bared.
As the world transforms, pure and bright,
In frosty whimsy, hearts take flight.

The Untold of the Silent Night

Beneath the stars, the world is still,
Secrets linger, hearts to fill.
In the dark, stories unfold,
Whispers of the brave and bold.

The moon keeps watch, a silver guide,
Echoes of dreams that cannot hide.
In quiet moments, truths arise,
The untold hidden in the skies.

Crickets sing their lullabies,
While shadows dance, the night complies.
Every heartbeat, a tale to share,
In the stillness, love lays bare.

Through frosty panes, the world reflects,
In this night, our soul connects.
Stars twinkle, a cherished sight,
Revealing all the untold light.

So hold this time, let silence reign,
For in the quiet, we gain.
The depths of night hold truth so bright,
In the untold of the silent night.

Silent Stories in the Frost

Whispers of winter softly creep,
Tales in silence, secrets to keep.
Each flake a memory to embrace,
In icy realms, we find our place.

Glistening trees with icy lace,
Nature's canvas, a frozen space.
Footprints lingering in the white,
Tell of wanderers lost to night.

Beneath the stars, stories unfold,
In silent echoes, mysteries told.
The frost holds wonders, dark and bright,
In twilight's grasp, we find the light.

Each dawn reveals a world anew,
With shimmering hues in every view.
Silent stories linger long,
In the frost's embrace, we belong.

When the sun bids the frost goodbye,
And colors blend in the morning sky,
The tales will fade, but hearts will know,
The silent stories in the snow.

Echoes of the Cold Sun

A chill awakens the day anew,
Where shadows dance in shades of blue.
The sun, a ghost, in skies so gray,
Whispers warmth to the cold, away.

Frosted branches, a glistening sight,
Mirror the sun's feeble light.
Each echo lingers, soft and low,
Resonates with the falling snow.

Footsteps crunch on the frozen ground,
In this stillness, peace is found.
The world is quiet, breath held tight,
Awaiting warmth to set it right.

Moments freeze in the winter's hand,
Dreams float gently over this land.
The cold sun beams in muted grace,
Guiding us through this frosty place.

As dusk descends with a heavy sigh,
The echoes of day begin to die.
In the silence, our hopes will bloom,
Carried forth in the coming gloom.

The Calm Before the Thaw

Stillness rests on the winter's breath,
A world wrapped tight in the shroud of death.
Waiting patiently for life to break,
In the hush, a promise we partake.

Clouds knit together, a blanket drawn,
Holding tightly, the fragile dawn.
The frozen ground, a dormant seed,
Hiding dreams that spring will feed.

Whispering winds through barren trees,
Softly carry the hints of ease.
In quiet moments, hearts grow bold,
As the tale of the thaw unfolds.

Each passing hour, the tension swells,
Nature's rhythm, a secret tells.
The calm is heavy, yet sweetly light,
Preparing for warmth to chase the night.

Beneath the frost, life stirs anew,
Awakening senses, a vibrant hue.
The calm before the end of chill,
Is but a pause, a heart to fill.

Veiled in Frost

A crystal veil drapes the land,
Whispers linger, unplanned.
Nature's frosty artistry,
Veiling wonders, ever free.

Morning glows with silver light,
Hiding stories from the night.
Each breath seen in icy air,
Moments frozen, yet so rare.

The world transformed in white and gray,
Where spirit dances, come what may.
In this hush, a song takes flight,
Veiled in frost, hearts feel light.

Time slows down in winter's charm,
Nature's beauty, calm and warm.
A serene spell cast on the earth,
Veiled in frost, we find rebirth.

As sunlight breaks through, we rejoice,
In the warmth, the frost's soft voice.
With every thaw, new dreams are found,
In a world of wonder, we are bound.

Beneath a Winter's Cloak

Snowflakes whisper through the night,
Covering the earth in white.
Silent woods, a tranquil sight,
Beneath the stars, so soft, so bright.

Frozen streams in quiet sleep,
Nature's breath is cold and deep.
Branches bow, the silence keeps,
In winter's arms, the world will weep.

Moonlight dances on the ground,
A silver path, no sound around.
Footprints lead where dreams are found,
In the magic, hearts unbound.

Emerging light begins to glow,
Spring whispers in the undertow.
Yet still we cherish winter's show,
Its beauty, timeless as the snow.

So let us tread with tender grace,
In winter's calm, we find our place.
Beneath a cloak of snow's embrace,
We find the joy, we find the space.

Tales from the Icy Edge

From frozen climes where shadows play,
Tales of ice begin to sway.
Whispers of the frost's ballet,
In every flake, a story's stay.

Mountains high, so steep and grand,
Guarding secrets of the land.
The icy edge beneath our hand,
Bore witness to the years unplanned.

Crisp winds carry echoes bold,
Of ancient glories yet untold.
Within the chill, the warmth we hold,
In icy breath, the truth unfolds.

Children laugh, their spirits free,
On slippery slopes, they glide with glee.
Each icy tale, a memory,
A fleeting time, a jubilee.

As twilight dims and night descends,
The icy tales, our hearts defend.
With every word that warmth transcends,
In winter's grip, old magic blends.

The Gentle Touch of Cold

A gentle touch upon the skin,
Cold caress, where dreams begin.
Beneath the frost, life stirs within,
A quiet pulse, a soft, thin din.

Leaves shiver in the nipping breeze,
Nature sighs, a moment seized.
In every corner, shadows tease,
As winter's breath becomes a wheeze.

Stars twinkle in the darkened sky,
Like diamonds shared, they catch the eye.
A hush that makes the heart comply,
In solitude, the night will sigh.

Icicles hang from rooftops high,
Silent sentinels in winter's cry.
Glistening like a lover's lie,
They promise warmth as time goes by.

With every dawn, the cold will fade,
Yet memories within us stayed.
The gentle touch, a timeless trade,
In frozen moments, dreams are laid.

Surfaces of Ice

Crystalline charm, the ice does gleam,
Reflecting light like a waking dream.
Upon its surface, stillness beams,
In frozen frames, life's fleeting themes.

Fingers trace the patterned lines,
Each crack might hide, the past designs.
Stories trapped in frozen signs,
In surfaces of ice, the heart aligns.

Beneath the sheen, the currents flow,
Life's hidden pulse, a soft aglow.
In frosty breaths, feelings grow,
As winter's magic starts to show.

Around the pond, the children glide,
On surfaces where dreams reside.
With every spin, they laugh and bide,
A world of wonder, hearts collide.

Yet winter wanes, the thaw is near,
The surfaces will soon adhere.
But memories of joy held dear,
Are stitched in ice, forever clear.

Murmurs of the Hidden Glen

In the quiet shade of trees,
Soft whispers play with the breeze.
Gentle streams weave through the land,
Secrets shared, both wild and grand.

Beneath the canopy so green,
Nature's canvas, pure and serene.
Footsteps echo, fade away,
Murmurs dance in light of day.

Every rustle, every sigh,
Tells a tale as time goes by.
In the stillness, hearts will dwell,
Listening close, we hear it well.

From flowers bright to shadows deep,
In this glen, our dreams we keep.
As twilight falls, the stars ignite,
Murmurs linger in the night.

Here, the world can drift afar,
In the glen, beneath each star.
Breath of nature, soft and sweet,
Murmurs guide us on our feet.

The Serenity of Subzero

A blanket wrapped in purest white,
Silent world, a wondrous sight.
Whispers hang in icy air,
Nature's peace beyond compare.

Frosty trees in still repose,
Every flake a tale bestows.
Calm descends, the world asleep,
Amidst the chill, our hearts do leap.

Footprints crunch on snow so pure,
In frozen beauty, we endure.
Winter's breath, a gentle sigh,
In this realm, we dream and fly.

Stars above like diamonds gleam,
Shimmering like a distant dream.
Underneath the moon's soft glow,
Serenity in every snow.

Beneath the vast and frosty dome,
In this stillness, we find home.
A tranquil heart, forever free,
In subzero's serenity.

Frost-laden Fantasies

In the twilight, visions glow,
Sparkling frost like magic's show.
Each creation, a work of art,
From winter's breath, they spring to start.

Snowflakes twirl in a dance so light,
Casting dreams in silver light.
Whispers of frost in the air,
Painting landscapes rich and rare.

Beneath the eaves, the crystals hang,
Nature's lullaby softly sang.
Every branch, a story spun,
In this wonderland, we run.

Glistening fields where snowflakes play,
Chasing thoughts that drift away.
Frost-laden dreams encompass all,
In winter's grasp, we rise and fall.

With every breath, enchantments grow,
In this realm where visions flow.
Fantasies in winter's clasp,
In frosty dreams, we gently gasp.

Traces of a Winter's Kiss

Upon the ground, a shimmer lies,
Echoes soft beneath the skies.
Footprints left in snow's embrace,
Here we linger, here we trace.

Kissed by winter's gentle hand,
Nature's beauty, still and grand.
Crystalline tears we find and keep,
In frosty silence, secrets seep.

Branches bow with heavy grace,
Winter's touch, a sweet embrace.
Every flake, a fleeting glide,
Whispers linger, side by side.

Time slips softly, draped in white,
In this realm, all feels so right.
Moments cherished, dreams awake,
In this soft, enchanted break.

Underneath the pale moonbeam,
Life unfolds like a waking dream.
Traces left by winter's bliss,
In our hearts, a gentle kiss.

Under the Veil of Snow

Whispers dance on winter's breath,
Softly blanketing the earth,
A hush falls deep, a quiet death,
In the stillness, dreams give birth.

Beneath the white, the world transforms,
Trees wear coats of crystal lace,
Nature's canvas, beauty forms,
In each flake, a hidden grace.

Footprints trace a silent path,
Through the frosted, peaceful land,
Echoes of a gentle laugh,
In this realm, all time is spanned.

Stars peer through the chilly night,
Casting glimmers on the snow,
Guiding hearts with tender light,
In their glow, old memories flow.

Underneath the moon's soft glow,
Secrets linger, softly known,
In the magic of the snow,
A world wrapped in dreams has grown.

Dreams Wrapped in Ice

On frozen lakes, reflections gleam,
A tapestry of quiet dreams,
Where shadows dance and silence beams,
In this moment, nothing seems.

Crystal branches, shimmer bright,
Held in winter's firm embrace,
Whispers travel through the night,
Finding solace in this space.

Each breath puffs in frosty air,
As the stars begin to shine,
Woven tales beyond compare,
In the stillness, hearts entwine.

Icicles hang like silver threads,
Adorning eaves with frozen lace,
In this realm where sorrow treads,
Hope emerges, slow-paced grace.

Wrapped in layers of pure dreams,
A kaleidoscope of night,
Reality may tear at seams,
But in dreams, we find our light.

Glistening Veils of Twilight

As day departs and night takes flight,
Glistening veils drape the sky,
A mingling of dusk's soft light,
With whispers of stars passing by.

Hues of purple, hues of gold,
Blend together in a dance,
Stories of the day retold,
In this fleeting, gentle trance.

Leaves rustle in the cooling breeze,
Echoes of the day's warm cheer,
Nature pauses, bends the knees,
In the twilight's embrace, so near.

A canvas painted with soft sighs,
Where nightingale's sweet serenades,
Linger under starlit skies,
In whispers, all the world cascades.

Time slows down in twilight's hue,
Moments stretch, then softly cease,
In the quiet, dreams come true,
Wrapped in peace, a sweet release.

Cold Shadows of Yesterday

Echoes linger in the frost,
Whispers of what once was bright,
Memories of what love lost,
Cling to silence, holding tight.

In shadows cast by fading light,
Stories breathe from every wall,
Caressing breezes hold the night,
In their grasp, the past stands tall.

Footsteps mark the fading trail,
Tracing paths where laughter soared,
Yet in the wind, a fragile wail,
Tells of dreams that once adored.

The chill wraps around the heart,
Like the cloak of winter's chill,
Each moment feels like a fresh start,
Yet shadows linger, haunting still.

In the cold, a warmth remains,
Though time may steal the sun's embrace,
Amidst the shadows, hope sustains,
Finding light in the darkest place.

Shadows of the Season

In twilight's grasp, the world doth fade,
Leaves whisper tales of summer's jade.
Crisp air carries an autumn's sigh,
As daylight bows and shadows lie.

Against the dusk, the branches sway,
Holding secrets of the day.
A harvest moon begins to rise,
Casting glow on silent cries.

The earth prepares for winter's chill,
As nature pauses, calm and still.
Colors blend in fading light,
A canvas drawn in soft twilight.

With each breeze, a memory stirs,
Echoes linger, time purrs.
For seasons turn, but we remain,
Bound by love, marked by pain.

In shadows deep, our dreams entwine,
A dance of time, both yours and mine.
As autumn yields to winter's call,
We find our warmth in shadows tall.

The Quiet Embrace

In morning mist, the silence speaks,
A soft caress, where stillness leaks.
Upon the dawn, the world awakes,
In tender light, the darkness shakes.

The gentle touch of softest dew,
In moments brief, our hearts renew.
Beneath the sky, so vast and blue,
A quiet bond, just me and you.

We walk the path of clipped grass blades,
Where sunlight filters, softly fades.
In every glance, a story spun,
Our whispered dreams, like threads, are one.

Amidst the noise of lives around,
Your heartbeat makes the sweetest sound.
In shadows cast by leafy trees,
We find our peace, our memories.

The quiet moments between the beats,
Where laughter blooms and stillness meets.
In every sigh, a love embraced,
In every pause, our hearts are placed.

Frostbitten Memories

In winter's grip, the world grows still,
Each breath a cloud, a heart to fill.
The landscape glows with icy grace,
Past whispers haunt this frozen place.

Branches bare, like fingers extend,
Reach to the sky, the seasons mend.
Footsteps echo on silent streets,
A haunting tune the cold repeats.

Moonlight dances on fields of white,
Illuminating echoes of night.
Frostbitten dreams lay under snow,
In slumber's hold, the memories flow.

A fire crackles, warm and bright,
A refuge found in the coldest night.
We gather close, the past in our hands,
In stories woven like winter bands.

The chill may bite, yet love remains,
In frostbitten hearts, no loss, no gains.
Through every storm, we find our way,
In winter's clasp, forever stay.

Whispers Among Pines

Beneath the pines, where shadows dwell,
The wind weaves secrets, soft as a spell.
In rustling leaves, a gentle song,
Nature's voice, where we belong.

The forest breathes in quiet tones,
Among the trees, a heart finds homes.
Each whisper floats like feathered dreams,
In sunlit glades, where silence beams.

The scent of earth, so rich and deep,
In every corner memories creep.
A world untouched by hurried haste,
In tranquil trails, our fears erased.

With every step, the forest glows,
In shadows cast, a friendship grows.
In laughter shared, beneath the sky,
The ancient pines stand, ever nigh.

A tapestry of time unfurls,
In whispered sighs, our hearts are twirled.
Among the pines, our souls embrace,
For in this realm, we find our place.

Crystalline Thoughts in the Chill

In the stillness of the night,
Thoughts like snowflakes softly fall.
Glistening under moon's soft light,
Whispers echo through the hall.

Frosty breath hangs in the air,
Dreams crystallize, pure and bright.
Each heartbeat, a fleeting prayer,
Warmed by the hearth's gentle light.

Nature's canvas, bare and white,
Blankets earth in quiet grace.
With each star, a wondrous sight,
Tranquility finds its place.

In this realm where silence sings,
Crisp and clear the world unfolds.
A tapestry of glistening,
Warmth envelops as night holds.

Carved in ice, the stories stay,
Echoes of the past remain.
Through crystalline streets, we sway,
Winter's beauty, yet no pain.

Voices of the Wintry Woods

Whispers weave through frosty trees,
Nature's secrets softly shared.
Boughs adorned with icy keys,
Every leaf a tale declared.

Footsteps crunch on snowy ground,
In the hush, the world awakes.
Echoes of lost dreams resound,
Through the stillness, silence breaks.

Yet the whispers tell of hope,
Winter's heart beats strong and true.
Branches sway, in rhythm, cope,
Tales of warmth in frozen blue.

Carried on the chilled night breeze,
Messages from far away.
In their chorus, comfort flees,
From the grip of cold's display.

Softly now, the twilight glows,
Pink and gold across the skies.
In the woods, a magic flows,
Echoing the night's lullabies.

Frosty Footprints in Silence

In a world of hush and white,
Footprints mark the paths we tread.
Every step a silent flight,
Echoing where dreams have led.

Each corner holds a tale untold,
Traces of a fleeting glance.
Frosty fingers, bright and bold,
Nature's quiet, timeless dance.

Shadowed trails through frozen glen,
Memory wrapped in icy lace.
Every path we wander, when
Softly touched by winter's face.

The breath of night begins to fade,
Stars peek through the silver haze.
Footprints soon by frost obeyed,
Erased by morning's gentle rays.

Yet within our hearts remain,
The echoes of this chilly spell.
Frosty footprints leave a stain,
In silence where our stories dwell.

In the Grip of Winter's Silence

Wrapped in layers, warm and tight,
Winter envelopes like a dream.
Stars ignite the velvet night,
In their glow, the shadows beam.

Silence reigns among the trees,
Nature paused in contemplation.
Every breath a gentle breeze,
Whispers born of contemplation.

Frosty air, a canvas white,
Painting futures on the ground.
In the stillness, hearts take flight,
In the quiet, love is found.

Snowflakes dance with fleeting grace,
Caught in time, a twirling waltz.
Winter's grip, a soft embrace,
In the stillness, peace exalts.

As the dawn breaks cold and clear,
Winter's blessing, pure and kind.
In this grip, we find no fear,
Just the magic left behind.

Solstice Serenade

In the still of the night, shadows play,
Flickering stars in a celestial ballet.
Winter whispers in a hush so deep,
Awakening dreams as the world falls asleep.

Lights of the season dance in sight,
Celebrating solace, the longest night.
Gathered around, hearts beat as one,
Embracing the magic, a new day begun.

Fireside stories, laughter in the air,
Memories woven with love and care.
Nature's beauty, a canvas unfolds,
The solstice serenade softly told.

Stars like diamonds in an inky sea,
Reminding us all of who we can be.
Moments suspended, fragile yet bright,
In this sacred space, we find our light.

As the dawn kisses away the cold night,
A new adventure wakes with the light.
From now on, we'll hold this vow,
To cherish the magic, the here and now.

Threads of Silver in the Air

Morning sun spills gold on the ground,
Nature's symphony, a gentle sound.
Threads of silver in the air,
Weaving stories, a world so rare.

Leaves a-quiver, soft whispers breathe,
Tales of journeys, dreams we weave.
Each step taken, a dance with fate,
In this moment, we celebrate.

The sky blushes in shades of pink,
As we gather, pause, and think.
Connections formed, hearts intertwine,
In the threads of silver, we shine.

Clouds drift softly, shadows play,
Every heartbeat, a promise to stay.
Nature's embrace, a tranquil song,
In this tapestry, we all belong.

As day unfolds, we reach for more,
Dreams taking flight, hearts to explore.
Threads of silver guide our way,
Intertwined futures, come what may.

A Symphony of Snow and Silence

In the hush of snow, time stands still,
Whispers of winter, a gentle thrill.
Each flake that falls, an artful song,
Painting the world, lovely and strong.

The trees wear blankets of purest white,
Guardians of secrets kept through the night.
Footsteps muffled, a ghostly dance,
In this zen moment, we find our chance.

Breathe in the magic, savor the air,
A symphony crafted with delicate care.
Frozen melodies drift through the sky,
Echoes of beauty in every sigh.

As twilight descends, stars shimmer bright,
The canvas of evening, a wondrous sight.
Wrapped in stillness, as dreams take flight,
In the silence, we find our light.

Together we stand, in awe and in thrill,
Bound by the whispers, the quiet chill.
A symphony of moments, soft in refrain,
In snow's gentle embrace, we remain.

Glistening Memories of the Night

Moonlight dances on the ocean's face,
Glistening memories in time and space.
Whispers of stories, secrets to share,
Moments captured in the midnight air.

Stars above wink in a celestial play,
Guiding our hearts as we wander and sway.
Every breath taken, rich with delight,
In the stillness, the world feels right.

Echoes of laughter bounce off the sea,
In this together, you and me.
Painting the night with dreams entwined,
In glistening memories, treasures we find.

As shadows linger, horizons gleam,
Chasing the essence of every dream.
In moonlit silence, we find our way,
With every heartbeat, come what may.

So let's dance on the edge of the night,
With glistening memories, futures so bright.
Hold tight, dear friend, to the joys in our sight,
For in this moment, everything feels right.

In the Stillness of December

Silent nights draw near, the world in white,
Soft whispers of snowflakes dancing in light.
Each breath hangs heavy, a lull in the air,
December's stillness, a moment to share.

Fires blaze gently, casting warm glow,
Memories linger, in soft winter's flow.
Sipping on cocoa, with laughter we stay,
In the stillness of December, time seems to sway.

The chill paints the windows with frostbitten lace,
Children excited, their joy we embrace.
Footsteps are muffled, a hush on the street,
As dreams of the season gather our feet.

Night skies adorn with the stars shining bright,
Fragrant pine needles, a scent of the night.
Candles are lit, hope flickers anew,
In December's silence, our hearts remain true.

So let us remember these moments to hold,
As frost wraps the world in a shimmer of gold.
Together we cherish the magic and cheer,
In the stillness of December, love draws us near.

Frost-Kissed Dreams

Under the moonlight, dreams start to gleam,
Frost on the window, a delicate seam.
Whispers of winter float soft through the night,
In the quiet of slumber, all feels just right.

Leaves turned to silver, trees wear a crown,
Each glimmering moment brings joy, not a frown.
With stars as our guide, we wander through light,
Frost-kissed dreams blossom, enchanting the night.

Sleep under blankets of shimmering grace,
Morning will greet us with a warm embrace.
A tapestry woven from whispers of cold,
In frost-kissed dreams, new stories unfold.

Beneath the vast sky, we dance and we sway,
In this frozen embrace, we wish not to stray.
Each lingering sparkle, a wish we can keep,
Frost-kissed dreams cradle us softly to sleep.

As dawn paints the world in hues of soft blue,
We cherish the magic that frost always drew.
Together we wake to the beauty outside,
Frost-kissed dreams linger, where hearts open wide.

Beneath the Blanket of White

Under a blanket, so soft and so white,
The world finds its peace, in the hush of the night.
Snowflakes like whispers, fall gentle and light,
Beneath the white quilt, everything feels right.

Branches are laden with glistening lace,
Nature slows down in a warm, sweet embrace.
Footprints are hidden, the scene feels so bright,
Beneath the blanket, stars shimmer in sight.

Candles flicker softly, casting pure glow,
Each moment is cherished, like falling snow.
With laughter and stories, our hearts take flight,
Beneath the white wonder, love shines so bright.

The chill in the air brings a spark to the soul,
Each soft breath we share makes our spirits feel whole.
Together we gather, wrapped up in delight,
Beneath the blanket of white, everything's right.

So let us enjoy what this season will bring,
In the quiet of winter, our hearts start to sing.
Embracing the magic, our dreams take their height,
Beneath the blanket of white, love feels so bright.

Ethereal Drifts at Dusk

As dusk falls gently, the world turns to grey,
Ethereal drifts begin softly to play.
Whispers of twilight dance light on the ground,
In the hush of the evening, magic is found.

Fog wraps the branches, a mystical sight,
Stars peek from shadows, igniting the night.
Each breeze carries stories of dreams long ago,
Ethereal drifts weave a tale soft and low.

Crystals of ice glisten, each one a pearl,
Nature awakened, an enchanting swirl.
With hearts open wide, we breathe in the dusk,
Ethereal drifts whisper of hope, and of trust.

The sky blushes softly, hues blending anew,
Painting the canvas with shades bright and true.
Amidst the serenity, we find peace, we bask,
In ethereal drifts, our hearts gently ask.

So linger awhile in the glow of this scene,
Trust in the beauty that life can glean.
Let moments of wonder forever remain,
Ethereal drifts at dusk chase away all the pain.

Frosted Whispers

In the quiet dawn, frost lays its claim,
Whispers of winter, calling your name.
A delicate layer on branches and stone,
Nature's soft secrets, in silence, are shown.

Soft snowflakes flutter like dreams in the air,
Painting the world with a magical stare.
Footsteps are muffled on paths made of white,
As the day awakens, embracing the light.

The chill of the morning brings clarity bright,
Frosted whispers dance in the soft morning light.
Glimmers of beauty in every small glance,
Creating a world where we quietly dance.

Nature's soft breath, wrapped in a shroud,
Frosted whispers sing, gentle and loud.
Hearts feel the magic, the cold's sweet caress,
In the stillness of winter, we find our rest.

The Lullaby of Winter's Breath

Winter's breath sings a lullaby soft,
Cradling the world, as spirits lift off.
Snowflakes descend like notes from the sky,
Each falling whisper, a gentle goodbye.

Under the stars, the night cradles dreams,
The moon glimmers gently, casting calm beams.
Wrapped snug in blankets, we drift far away,
Carried by sounds of the night's sweet ballet.

Cool winds embrace with a soothing refrain,
Nature composing her delicate train.
Frost on the window paints stories in white,
As we listen close to the lull of the night.

Through darkened woods, the echoes do sigh,
Where branches weave tales beneath midnight sky.
The lullaby lingers, both tender and deep,
As winter's sweet promise lulls us to sleep.

A Quiet Dance with the Dark

Night drapes itself with a velvet embrace,
Stars twinkle softly, in their celestial race.
Whispers of shadows entwine with the light,
A quiet dance unfolds, a beautiful sight.

Trees sway gently, their branches like arms,
Cradling the stillness, enchanted by charms.
Moonlight spills silver on faces turned up,
As dreams and desires begin to erupt.

In the still of the night, hearts start to sway,
Lost in the music that guides us away.
Footsteps are silent, as whispers take flight,
In a quiet dance with the depths of the night.

Memories flicker like soft candle flames,
As we embrace moments, with no two the same.
Wrapped in the darkness, we find our sweet tune,
In the quiet of night, beneath the soft moon.

Hidden Stories in the Snowfall

Snowflakes gather, each one unique,
Telling of journeys, the stories we seek.
Beneath the white cover, whispers take form,
Hidden tales linger, through calmness and storm.

Footprints are carved in a blanket so pure,
Tracing our paths while the world feels demure.
Silent confessions ride on winter's breath,
A canvas of quiet, where secrets find death.

Branches hold stories of laughter and tears,
Echoing memories through the fleeting years.
With every snowfall, the past drifts away,
Yet the whispers of history choose to stay.

Through flurries of white, our hearts come alive,
In the silence of snowfall, lost tales survive.
Embraced by the frost, they linger in time,
Hope woven gently in rhythm and rhyme.

Silent Snowflakes

Silent snowflakes gently fall,
Dancing like whispers, soft and small.
Blanketing earth in purest white,
Transforming the world, a serene sight.

Each flake unique, a crafted dream,
Cascading down in a glittering stream.
They hush the chaos, bring calm to night,
Under the moon, they shimmer bright.

A hush descends on the frosty ground,
Nature's quiet, a tranquil sound.
Footprints vanish, lost in their grace,
In silence vast, we find our place.

Winter's magic, a painter's touch,
Crafting beauty that we love so much.
In this snowfall, our worries drift,
With every flake, our spirits lift.

So let us cherish each fleeting hour,
Embrace the stillness, the chilling power.
For in the dance of silence and snow,
We find the warmth in the cold winds' blow.

Murmurs in the Frost

Murmurs in the frostbite air,
Subtle secrets everywhere.
Trees adorned in icy lace,
Nature whispers, finds its grace.

Each breath released, a vapor plume,
Echoes softly in the gloom.
The world pauses, takes a rest,
In the chill, we feel the best.

Frosty petals, crisp and clear,
Nature's calmness, drawing near.
With every crunch beneath our feet,
We find the quiet, the bittersweet.

Shadows stretch in the fading light,
As day surrenders to the night.
In whispered tones, the cold will sing,
Of the beauty that winter brings.

So linger long in the frosty air,
In the quiet, find your share.
For in these murmurs, life does flow,
In the frosty whispers of the snow.

Echoes of the Frostbite

Echoes of the frostbite chill,
Nights so silent, calm, and still.
Stars twinkle in the winter skies,
Reflecting dreams in our closed eyes.

Frosted windows, patterns divine,
Nature's artistry, a sign.
Each crystal formed a story tells,
In the biting cold, our heart swells.

Silent echoes through the trees,
Played by winds with gentle ease.
Branches bend, the world observes,
Winter's nature, it curves and swerves.

Chill wraps round like a soft embrace,
Time suspended in this space.
In frozen moments, we find peace,
As the echoes of the frostbite cease.

Cherish these hours, lost in the haze,
In winter's grip, we'll find our ways.
With every echo, we breathe anew,
In frost's embrace, love will ensue.

Chilled Breezes and Soft Shadows

Chilled breezes whisper through the night,
Carrying dreams in their flight.
Soft shadows dance on silver lanes,
Nature's rhythm, the heart's refrains.

With every gust, the world awakes,
A sigh that flutters, a moment shakes.
The stars glance down with a twinkling eye,
As breezes weave in a lullaby.

Cold embraces the quiet ground,
In stillness, the softest sounds.
The world is draped in winter's shawl,
In this deep calm, we feel it all.

Whispers of warmth found in the chill,
Murmurs that linger, a quiet thrill.
In shadows cast by the pale moonlight,
We find our solace, our hearts take flight.

So let the breezes play their tune,
Underneath the watchful moon.
In chilled whispers and soft strokes,
The heart unravels, the spirit awoke.

The Stillness of Night

The moon hangs high, a silver eye,
In shadows deep, where whispers sigh.
Stars twinkle softly, a distant choir,
While dreams alight on wings of fire.

Beneath the quilt of velvet skies,
Time drifts slow, like lullabies.
In every heart a secret spark,
Igniting hope within the dark.

Trees sway gently, in silent dance,
As night unfolds its mystic chance.
Every breeze carries a tale,
Of wonders found on night's vast scale.

Yet in this peace, a pulse remains,
A world awakes beneath the chains.
With every breath, the night grows bold,
In stillness, all the dreams unfold.

So let us dwell in twilight's grace,
Where shadows move and time finds pace.
In the stillness of the night we find,
The gentle echoes of the mind.

Frost-kissed Dreams

Morning breaks with glistening light,
Frost-kissed dreams in pure delight.
Each blade of grass wears diamonds bright,
As day unveils its radiant sight.

With every breath, the air is still,
A treasure found on winter's hill.
In each exhale, small clouds arise,
Painting patterns 'neath the skies.

The world transforms in icy hue,
With nature's hand, a canvas new.
Soft whispers float in crisp, clear air,
As dreams take flight without a care.

Childhood memories of snowflakes fall,
In every flurry, a gentle call.
To dance and play in frosty chills,
Awakens joy, where magic spills.

So let us cherish this fleeting scene,
Frost-kissed dreams in silver sheen.
For in each glimmer, we shall see,
The beauty of life's mystery.

Soft Cascades of White

Gentle whispers of winter's breath,
Blanket the earth in quiet depth.
Soft cascades of white cascade down,
Turning the world into a gown.

Every flake a unique design,
Dances through the air, divine.
They swirl and twirl, then softly land,
Creating wonders, hand in hand.

The trees wear coats of glistening lace,
In this magical, serene space.
Nature breathes a softened sigh,
As day drifts on, the hours fly.

Children laugh with joy untold,
Building castles, brave and bold.
In every flurry, hearts will soar,
Soft cascades of white, we adore.

So let us wander, hand in hand,
Through winter's beauty, wonderland.
With every step, a world anew,
In soft cascades of white, we view.

Enchanted in the Cold

Underneath a sky of gray,
Magic whispers, dreams away.
Snowflakes dance in twinkling light,
Enchanted moments, pure delight.

Barren trees stand tall and proud,
Shimmering softly, a silver shroud.
Nature's silence swathes the land,
Wrapped in peace by winter's hand.

Footprints crunch on frozen ground,
In this stillness, solace found.
Every breath brings frosty air,
A world transformed, beyond compare.

Wild shadows creep through drifts of white,
Where dreams ignite in the heart's light.
Enchanted whispers in the cold,
Stories of warmth waiting to unfold.

So gather close, let hearts unite,
For in this chill, all feels just right.
In every moment, a lesson told,
We find our joy, enchanted in the cold.

Hushed Tones of the Hearth

In the amber glow, shadows play,
Whispers of night begin to sway.
Flickering flames weave tales untold,
A warmth that wraps like threads of gold.

Old stories dance around the room,
Echoes of laughter dispelling gloom.
With every crackle, hearts entwine,
In this cocoon, the world's divine.

Smoke curls high, a silent vow,
In furnace warmth, we feel it now.
Moments cherished, time stands still,
In hushed tones, the heart does fill.

Tameless spirits come alive,
In the night, as dreams arrive.
A safe embrace, where souls ignite,
In the hearth's love, we find our light.

Softly whispers draw us near,
In tender warmth, we have no fear.
With every breath, we share our fate,
In hushed tones, we contemplate.

Crystalline Serenade

Dancing lights on a frosty morn,
Glistening gems, the day is born.
Crystal branches shimmer bright,
A serenade of pure delight.

Each flake drifts with silent grace,
A blanket white, the world's embrace.
Harmonies of silence make,
The heart leap with every quake.

Nature sings in hushed repose,
In every sound, a story grows.
A winter's whisper fills the air,
In crystalline magic, we repair.

Snowflakes twirling, pure and free,
Painting dreams for you and me.
Soft serenades of fleeting time,
In frozen moments, we climb.

The world transformed, a glacial show,
As nature's lullabies softly flow.
In each breath, a secret veiled,
In crystalline beauty, we're unveiled.

Snow-laden Secrets

Beneath the drift, a silence rests,
Buried dreams within the quests.
Hushed whispers ride on winter's breath,
Shrouded truths in the snow's caress.

Frozen trails in twilight's haze,
A realm where memory always stays.
Each step crunches with stories bold,
In snow-laden secrets, we find gold.

Frosted whispers beneath the pine,
Nature's canvas, pure and fine.
In every flake, a tale anew,
Snow-laden secrets shared with few.

The quiet earth, a blanket wide,
Bears witness to what hearts confide.
In winter's hold, we seek to know,
What lies beneath the sparkling snow.

In the stillness, echoes bloom,
A world awakened from its gloom.
Snow-laden whispers softly sweep,
In tranquil night, our hearts will leap.

The Art of Silent Falls

In twilight's hush, the world reveals,
A symphony of earth that heals.
Water cascades in tranquil grace,
The art of falls, a gentle embrace.

Misty veil wraps the landscape tight,
A quiet dance in fading light.
Each droplet sings a soft refrain,
In golden hues, we feel the rain.

Nature's whispers fill the air,
In every rush, we feel a prayer.
Silent falls, where spirits soar,
A sacred space we all adore.

Sculpted rocks, the canvas worn,
Lifetimes etched where love is born.
In still reflections, we find our way,
The art of silent falls at play.

From height to pool, the journey flows,
In tranquil depths, our solace grows.
We listen close as nature calls,
In harmony, the spirit sprawls.

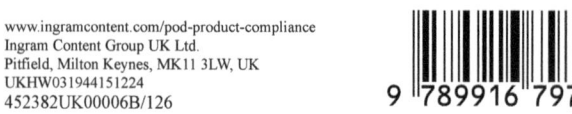

www.ingramcontent.com/pod-product-compliance
Ingram Content Group UK Ltd.
Pitfield, Milton Keynes, MK11 3LW, UK
UKHW031944151224
452382UK00006B/126